ALCOHOL & DRUG ABUSE

Breaking Free & Staying Free

JUNE HUNT

Torrance, California

Alcohol & Drug Abuse: Breaking Free & Staying Free

Aspire Press, a division of Rose Publishing, Inc.
4733 Torrance Blvd., #259
Torrance, California 90503 USA
www.aspirepress.com

Register your book at www.aspirepress.com/register
Get inspiration via email, sign up at www.aspirepress.com

The information and solutions offered in this resource are a result of years of Bible study, research, and practical life application. They are intended as guidelines for healthy living and are not a replacement for professional counseling or medical advice. JUNE HUNT and HOPE FOR THE HEART make no warranties, representations, or guarantees regarding any particular result or outcome. Any and all express or implied warranties are disclaimed. Please consult qualified medical, pastoral, and psychological professionals regarding individual conditions and needs. JUNE HUNT and HOPE FOR THE HEART do not advocate that you treat yourself or someone you know and disclaim any and all liability arising directly or indirectly from the information in this resource.

For more information on Hope For The Heart, visit www.hopefortheheart.org or call 1-800-488-HOPE (4673).

Printed by Regent Publishing Services Ltd.
Printed in China
November 2014, 3rd printing

CONTENTS

Dear friend,

I wish you had known my Uncle Billy. He was quite bright. His teachers said that he was the kind of student who could make straight A's without even coming to classes! He was handsome with dark brown hair and deep set dimples in both cheeks. Everyone wanted to be around Uncle Billy, but he wouldn't allow much closeness. He kept his distance.

Although my uncle was smart and capable, I always felt sorry for him because he was somewhat the "black sheep" of the family. By the time I was a teenager, Uncle Billy had gone through many tough times. One day he awakened to find out he had lost his small refrigerator-freezer business—his business partner ran off with his wife and all of the company's money. He was devastated.

His life loomed as a dark picture of losses. He lost his wife, his business, his health, and his self-respect. He completely lost control of his life because something else had control of him. And ultimately he lost his life. You see, my Uncle Billy was an alcoholic, and he died as a result of suicide. We all loved Uncle Billy, but in the end we lost him.

I have often wondered, *What could have helped my Uncle Billy? What could have saved him from his own self-destruction?* Like my uncle's, countless other lives have been destroyed by a chemical addiction, leaving family and friends struggling with similar questions: *What set up this struggle with substance abuse? What could I have done to help?*

With addictions affecting so many, you may be wondering, *Can those in the throes of a chemical dependency be set free—permanently?* The answer is *yes*! There is hope. In order to break free from an addiction, there must first be the recognition that there is a problem and the willingness to face the problem so that healing can take place. But the most important step is turning to God, allowing His strength to help carry the burden. Isaiah 41:13 says, *"For I am the LORD, your God, who takes hold of your right hand and says to you, Do not fear; I will help you."*

If you are struggling with a chemical addiction, the heavenly Father is waiting for you with open arms, beckoning you to come to Him. He will walk with you each step of the way in your journey to freedom. Like His prodigal son who *"was lost and has been found"* (Luke 15:32 NASB)—you need not be lost anymore.

Yours in the Lord's hope,

June

June Hunt

ALCOHOL & DRUG ABUSE

Breaking Free & Staying Free

He was an all-American hero. Some say he was the greatest baseball player who ever lived.[1] Mickey Mantle seemed to have it all—fame, fortune, and millions of fans. The day of his graduation from high school in 1950, he signed with the world renowned New York Yankees, a decision that began his road to stardom. The statistics support his superstar status: 536 career home runs, three Most Valuable Player awards, a career batting average of .298, seven World Championships, and baseball's Triple Crown, meaning he led the entire major league in the three categories of highest batting average, most home runs, and most runs batted in.

However, Mickey also lived an extravagant, alcoholic lifestyle filled with various types of abuse. When he was diagnosed with liver cancer, it was evident that the years of drinking had intensified the damage. Despite his successful treatment for alcoholism, the assault to his body was too severe, and death came swiftly. During the final inning of his life, Mickey stood before the microphones at a press conference, gestured toward himself, wanting the world to know that he was no role model, and said, "Don't be like me."[2]

What could take the greatest switch-hitter in the game of baseball from adoration down to addiction? Why do millions of people each year take that same painful path? The Bible gives this explanation:

"There is a way that seems right to a man, but in the end it leads to death." (Proverbs 16:25)

DEFINITIONS

What is a drug?[3]

- A drug is a chemical substance introduced into the body that produces physical, emotional, or mental changes. Some drugs are helpful, and some are harmful.

Three primary ways of using drugs:

- Ingesting—swallowing pills, powders, liquids
- Inhaling—breathing in powders, smoke, fumes, and other inhalants
- Injecting—inserting a substance directly into the veins, which provides a more direct effect, or injecting the drug underneath the skin (called "skin popping"), which allows the drug to be absorbed more slowly into the blood stream

Three ways of obtaining drugs:

- Over-the-counter (including alcohol)
- Prescription (only prescribed by a medical doctor)
- Illegally (The legal status of a drug varies from country to country.)

QUESTION: "Is it possible to abuse drugs and alcohol and not become addicted?"

ANSWER: Yes. Just as every drug is different, everyone's physical makeup is different. Some people become addicted after small amounts of a substance; others consume greater quantities before becoming dependent. Because of the destructive risk of addiction, using unnecessary drugs is dangerous. Substance abuse is like playing Russian roulette—it can cost you your life.

Conscientious Christians need to know that our bodies are not our own to abuse in any way—they belong to God.

"Do you not know that your body is a temple of the Holy Spirit, who is in you, whom you have received from God? You are not your own; you were bought at a price. Therefore honor God with your body."
(1 Corinthians 6:19–20)

WHAT IS Substance Abuse?[4]

Substance abuse is the use of a chemical, legal or illegal, to the point of causing a person physical, mental, or emotional harm.

There are five types of substance abusers.

- An ***experimental*** user is a person who uses a drug out of curiosity.
- A ***recreational*** user is a person who "gets high" on drugs on special occasions (parties, celebrations).
- A ***regular*** user is a person in a constant pattern of drug abuse who also attempts to live a normal lifestyle.
- A ***binge*** user is a person who uses drugs uncontrollably for a brief period of time and then abstains until the next binge.
- A ***dependent*** user is a person who is emotionally and physically hooked on drugs and whose life centers around obtaining those drugs. This person has a chemical dependency.

Regardless of the substance, the Bible describes the substance abuser: "*When such a person hears the words of this oath, he invokes a blessing on himself and therefore thinks, 'I will be safe, even though I persist in going my own way.' This will bring disaster on the watered land as well as the dry*" (Deuteronomy 29:19).

QUESTION: "I have friends who drink heavily—sometimes to excess—and they want me to party with them. Is it okay for me to go with them, even if I am not drinking?"

ANSWER: There's an old saying, "You become like what you hang around with" or, as the Bible says, *"Bad company corrupts good morals"* (1 Corinthians 15:33 NASB). Going with those friends is not wise. Scripture clearly states,

> **"Do not join those who drink too much wine or gorge themselves on meat."**
> **(Proverbs 23:20)**

WHAT ARE the Four Major Drug Classifications?[5]

Drugs are generally classified into four major groups depending on their effect on the body.

1. **Depressants** are drugs that produce a calming effect and slow down the central nervous system.

   - Prevalent types are alcohol, sedatives (sleeping pills), tranquilizers (valium), barbiturates ("downers"), and organic solvents (model airplane glue, gasoline, and aerosols).

   - Psychological symptoms are poor concentration, distorted thinking, lack of judgment, and aggressiveness.

- Physical effects are drowsiness, slurred speech, lack of coordination, tremors, decreased energy, coma, impaired vision, decreased pulse rate and blood pressure, respiratory depression, and death.

The Bible refers to those who ...

"Stagger from wine and reel from beer ... and are befuddled with wine; they reel from beer, they stagger when seeing visions, they stumble when rendering decisions." (Isaiah 28:7)

2 **Stimulants** are drugs that excite bodily functions and speed up the central nervous system.

- Prevalent types are cocaine, crack, meth, and amphetamines ("speed" or "uppers").
- Psychological symptoms are excitability, increased energy, exaggerated self-confidence, heightened sexual drives, temporary exhilaration, irritability, apprehension, and intensification of all emotions.
- Physical effects are hyperactivity, restlessness, insomnia, loss of appetite, dry mouth, bad breath, itchy nose, dilated pupils, rapid and unclear speech, perspiration, headaches, dizziness, elevated blood pressure and heart rate, psychosis, and death.

The book of Proverbs describes those who walk without wisdom, those who are victims of their own folly. Like the one who takes stimulants ...

"Disaster will overtake him in an instant; he will suddenly be destroyed—without remedy." (Proverbs 6:15)

3 **Hallucinogens** are drugs that alter and distort reality.

- Prevalent types are LSD, marijuana, PCP ("angel dust"), and mescaline.
- Psychological symptoms are hallucinations, heightened sensitivities, anxiety attacks, lowered inhibitions, and out-of-body experiences.
- Physical effects vary with each drug. LSD acts as a stimulant; marijuana acts as a depressant (reactions differ with each individual): sleeplessness, loss of appetite, increased energy, increased pulse rate and blood pressure, eyes fixed in a blank stare or rapid involuntary eye movements, slurred or blocked speech, higher rate of accidents and violence, disorientations, and death.

Although the Bible does not directly mention hallucinogens, it does address the hallucinogenic effect of alcohol, which is frightening and disturbing.

"Your eyes will see strange sights and your mind imagine confusing things. You will be like one sleeping on the high seas, lying on top of the rigging. 'They hit me,' you will say, 'but I'm not hurt! They beat me, but I don't feel it! When will I wake up so I can find another drink?'"
(Proverbs 23:33–35)

4 **Narcotics** are drugs that reduce pain and elevate a person's mood.

- Prevalent types are opium, morphine, codeine, heroin, methadone, and meperidine.
- Psychological symptoms are temporary euphoria, dulled senses, lethargy, and confusion.
- Physical effects are relief of pain, droopy eyelids, constricted pupils, slowed reaction and motor skills, drowsiness, lack of coordination, depressed reflexes, dry mouth, constipation, scars or abscesses at injection sites, and death.

When you are in pain, rather than turning to drugs, turn to the Lord, be dependent on Him, and seek His direction for pain relief.

"I am in pain and distress; may your salvation, O God, protect me."
(Psalm 69:29)

WHAT IS the Downward Spiral of Dependency?

You may start by thinking that a drug serves you, but to think that a drug is serving you is to have a "tiger by the tail." It will inevitably turn on you. Do not be deceived: The drug that serves you today will own you tomorrow.[6]

> **"Do not let sin reign in your mortal body so that you obey its evil desires." (Romans 6:12)**

- **Intoxication** occurs when the influence of a substance in your body causes changes in your behavior, including mood changes, faulty judgment, slurred speech, poor coordination, unsteady gait, sexual impropriety, aggressive behavior, and impaired social functioning. Intoxication may result in becoming comatose or even in death.
  - *Dorland's Medical Dictionary* defines *intoxication* as "poisoning; the state of being poisoned."[7] How interesting that Moses said, "*Their grapes are filled with poison. ... Their wine is the venom of serpents, the deadly poison of cobras*" (Deuteronomy 32:32–33).
- **Abuse** occurs when your use of drugs results in your failure to fulfill responsibilities or to maintain healthy relationships or when you put yourself or others at risk of potential harm.

- **Addiction** occurs when you experience these three leading indicators:
  - ***Drug tolerance.*** You need increasingly more to obtain the same effect.
  - ***Physical dependence.*** You suffer from withdrawal symptoms such as nausea, sweating, shaking, and anxiety.
  - ***Craving.*** You develop a pattern of compulsive drug use.

  Other common indicators include:

  - Failing at attempts to control or decrease your substance abuse
  - Spending your time targeting activities to obtain, use, or recover from the effects of the substance
  - Reducing or abandoning your meaningful social, work, or recreational activities
  - Continuing to use the substance despite recurring physical or psychological problems

- **Withdrawal** occurs when the distress caused by a lessening or lack of the drug severely disrupts your daily life.

The Bible describes a distressing time when ...

> **…nger do they drink wine with a song.**
> **…ts they cry out for wine; all joy**
> **…m, all gaiety is banished."**
> **(Isaiah 24:9, 11)**

QUESTION: "How can I be held responsible for my drug dependence since most drugs are addictive and actually cause the addiction?"

ANSWER: Your drug dependence has been created both by your choice to use drugs and by the drug itself. Intoxication results from the makeup of the drug you use and the way it is metabolized by your body. The only way to avoid addiction is to choose to stop abusing drugs.

"How long will you keep on getting drunk? Get rid of your wine."
(1 Samuel 1:14)

WHAT IS Codependency?

A word often associated with chemical dependency and the dysfunctional relationships that accompany drug abuse is the term *codependency.*

- The word *codependent* was first used in the 1970s to describe a family member living *with* someone dependent on alcohol, the alcoholic. The prefix *co-* means "with" or "one associated with the action of another."
- The codependent person or "enabler" enables the alcoholic to continue with the addiction without drawing and maintaining boundaries.
- The word *codependency* became a term describing the dysfunctional behavior of family members seeking to adapt to the alcoholic's negative behavior. The dynamic of codependency is similar to that of having an elephant in the living room that no one talks about, but everyone maneuvers around in such a way that the elephant will cause as little disruption as possible.
- Codependency is a relationship addiction. Just as the alcoholic is dependent on alcohol, the codependent is overly dependent on the relationship with the alcoholic.
- Today, the word *codependent* refers to anyone who is dependent on another to the point of being controlled or manipulated by that person.

QUESTION: "How can I know whether I am being an enabler?"

ANSWER: You are an enabler if you perpetuate another's substance abuse by protecting that person from painful consequences that could actually serve as a motivation for change.

For example, a passive parent allows the daughter's drug abuse to continue—even to the detriment of other family members. Or the codependent wife calls her husband's boss to say he has the flu, when instead he has a hangover.[8] Ask yourself, "How many lies have I told to protect the reputation of the one I love?"

The Bible has strong words about those who protect the guilty:

> **"Whoever says to the guilty, 'You are innocent'—peoples will curse him."**
> **(Proverbs 24:24)**

CHARACTERISTICS OF SUBSTANCE ABUSE

When the fans saw Mickey Mantle—a power hitter with the speed of a sprinter—they were in awe. Yet did the average fan see the symptoms of the alcoholism? Most did not, but his family did.

Mickey's children spoke of his increasing inattention to his family while they were young. He became more depressed, more irritable. When the Yankees lost a game or when Mickey struck out, the children knew to leave their dad alone. The entire family walked on eggshells, hoping to prevent the inevitable verbal abuse. Not only was Mickey in denial about his alcoholism, but his wife also minimized the problem.

Mantle made excuses for his absences, which often included time spent with other women. His increasing use of alcohol was a desperate attempt to boost his self-esteem. More and more, alcohol was necessary for him to function during the day; then more and more it became necessary in order for him to sleep at night.

A therapist once commented, "Mickey is totally controlled by fear. He is filled with fear about everything."[9] Mickey himself stated, "I am embarrassed by what I did when I drank: the foul language, the rudeness, having to face people the next day that I didn't remember insulting the night before."[10] No wonder he had fear.

Mickey lived out the second part of this Scripture:

**"Those who sleep, sleep at night, and those who get drunk, get drunk at night."
(1 Thessalonians 5:7)**

WHAT ARE the Warning Signs?

Mickey Mantle showed typical symptoms of addiction, yet from time to time we all feel depressed or may be inattentive to our families. When do certain characteristics become signs of an addiction? For a substance abuser, a combination of many symptoms can be observed—symptoms that fall into all four of these categories: *emotional*, *physical*, *behavioral*, and *spiritual*.

Emotional	
Unpredictable mood swings	Guilt
Depression	Shame
Fear of rejection	Anger
Frustration over little things	Anxiety

Notice this warning from Jesus in which He gives a graphic consequence: *"Be careful, or your hearts will be weighed down with dissipation, drunkenness and the anxieties of life, and that day will close on you unexpectedly like a trap"* (Luke 21:34).

Physical	
Poor general health	Loss of sexual desire
Shaky hands	Tendency to look older
Night sweats	Weight gain or puffiness
Bloodshot eyes	Unhealthy looking complexion

Again the Bible describes the addict: "*Who has woe? Who has sorrow? ... Who has bloodshot eyes? Those who linger over wine, who go to sample bowls of mixed wine*" (Proverbs 23:29–30).

Behavioral	
Secretiveness	Attempting to hide behavior
Exclusiveness	Associating only with other users
Compulsiveness	Responding as though the drug is absolutely necessary
Defensiveness	Shifting blame to others
Denial	Refusing to admit there is a problem
Dishonesty	Deceiving others about frequency of use and expenditure of money

Behavioral	
Weak/strong will	Being too weak to stop/too stubborn to get help
Rebelliousness	Refusing to act responsibly

The Bible even describes a self-indulgent alcoholic son: *"This son of ours is stubborn and rebellious. He will not obey us. He is a profligate and a drunkard"* (Deuteronomy 21:20).

Spiritual	
Feeling estranged from God	Diminished prayer life
Withdrawal from church life	Aversion to Scripture
Conviction by the Holy Spirit	Lack of joy
Fear of being disciplined by God	Hardened heart

The Lord describes those who choose to turn away from Him and instead choose "*new wine*": *"They do not cry out to me from their hearts but wail upon their beds. They gather together for grain and new wine but turn away from me"* (Hosea 7:14).

QUESTION: "What objective data can I give my teenager to discourage the use of alcohol or drugs?"

ANSWER: The Substance Abuse and Mental Health Services Administration's Summary for the year 2000 revealed that youths who use alcohol or drugs are more likely to commit suicide than youths who do not use.[11]

- Total (users and nonusers):
  - 9.4% of 12 to 13 year olds are at risk for suicide.
  - 13.7% of 14 to 17 year olds are at risk for suicide.
- With alcohol use:
  - 19.6% of youths who drink alcohol are at risk for suicide.
- With other drugs:
  - 25.4% of youths who use any illicit drug (including marijuana) are at risk for suicide.
  - 29.4% of youths who use any illicit drug except marijuana are at risk for suicide.

Be aware that the Bible says ...

"The righteousness of the upright delivers them, but the unfaithful are trapped by evil desires." (Proverbs 11:6)

CHECKLIST FOR Discovering a Chemical Dependency[12]

Had Mickey Mantle—or his family and friends—examined his drinking pattern in light of the following checklist, his addiction to alcohol would have been clearly seen and recognized years before it came to light.

C Do I ever attempt to ***conceal*** my habit from others?

H Do I ever think about getting ***help*** for my habit?

E Do I ever have problems at my place of ***employment*** because of my habit?

M Do I ever experience a loss of ***memory*** related to my habit?

I Do I ever become severely ***intoxicated***?

C Do I ever feel unfairly ***criticized*** because of my habit?

A Do I ever feel my habit is ***abnormal***?

L Do I ever ***lose*** friendships or have relationships as a result of my habit?

L Do I ever ***lower*** my intake but then return to my previous level of consumption?

Y Do I ever neglect my ***young*** ones or other loved ones because of my habit?

D Do I become ***defensive*** or argumentative about my use?

E Do I fail to get in touch with my ***emotions*** because of my use?

P Is my ***physical*** health affected by my use?

E Do I ***enjoy*** only functions where alcohol or other drugs are available?

N Is my ***need*** for the substance affecting my finances?

D Do I ***deny*** that I experience any consequences from my habit?

E Do I ***evade*** difficult situations by indulging in my habit?

N Is my ***need*** to feed my habit affecting my relationships?

T Is my ***tolerance*** level for the substance getting higher?

If you answered *yes* to five or more of the above questions, you may have a serious dependency.

If Mickey had acknowledged his alcoholism and received treatment early in his career, his title of *hero* to thousands of youngsters and *champion* of baseball would not have been marred by subsequent years of drinking.

"Woe to those who are heroes at drinking wine and champions at mixing drinks."
(Isaiah 5:22)

QUESTION: "If I am a habitual, compulsive drinker and drug user, can I really change and permanently stop?"

ANSWER: All habits, compulsions, and addictions are highly resistant and are therefore very difficult to change, yet not impossibly so. Repeating actions actually alters the brain, making it more difficult to change a pattern of choices. New patterns of behavior, however, can be learned. If you are a true believer, you have His Word to change your way of thinking, His church with specialized community groups to support your life change, and His Spirit to empower you from within to follow through to stop drinking.

"It is God who works in you to will and to act according to his good purpose." (Philippians 2:13)

WHAT CLUES Come from Chemically Dependent Kids?[13]

If you observe 50% or more of the following signs and symptoms of drug use in your teenager, it is likely that your teen is involved in harmful substance abuse—typically with friends. Pray for wisdom to recognize whether your teenager is in trouble, and tell your teen ...

"You may be sure that your sin will find you out."
(Numbers 32:23)

School

- Drop in grades
- Drowsiness/sleeping in class
- Tardiness, skipping classes, truancy
- Forging parents' signature on excuses
- Breaking the rules/breaking the law
- In-school suspensions, alternative school referral
- Shortened attention span, difficulty concentrating
- New set of friends in school or out of school
- Dropping out of once valued extracurricular activities

Personal

- Moody, irritable
- Agitated, angry, hostile
- Short- or long-term memory loss
- Unmotivated, lethargic, undisciplined
- Change in appearance, posture, grooming
- Change in appetite, eating more but consistently losing weight
- Looking unhealthy, bloodshot eyes, enlarged pupils, nagging cough
- Experiencing frequent skin and respiratory infections
- Sexually promiscuous, irregular menstrual cycles

Home

- Withdrawn, indifferent
- Argumentative, disrespectful, rude
- Using obscene or profane language
- Quiet and defensive about new friends
- Taking money and valuables from house
- Using air fresheners to cover up drug odors
- Decorating bedroom with posters of rock groups and drug related slogans
- Collecting pipes, small containers, cigarette papers, or other drug related items

- Leaving peculiar smelling cigarette butts, seeds, or leaves in ashtrays or pant pockets

The Bible gives this general warning to young people who walk without wisdom:

"He will die for lack of discipline, led astray by his own great folly." (Proverbs 5:23)

Note: If either you or your son or daughter is experiencing these symptoms, be sure to consult your health-care professional.

QUESTION: "What should I do? Recently my teenage daughter swore me to secrecy before telling me that my son-in-law had offered her illegal drugs. Although she refused the drugs, she is adamant about my not saying anything because she doesn't want to 'cause a problem.'"

ANSWER: You already have a problem! Right now, you must consider what is in the best interest of your daughter. She should be protected by relatives, not tempted by them. Tell your daughter that you don't have the peace of God about keeping this confidence because your son-in-law's actions have betrayed the family bond. Let her know that you must confront him because, instead of violating family boundaries, he needs to respect them. Explain to your daughter that confronting the truth could open his eyes and ultimately *save his life.*

"A truthful witness saves lives." (Proverbs 14:25)

WHAT CLUES Are Characteristic of Children with an Addicted Parent?

- **Guilt**—Does the child see himself or herself as the main cause of a parent's chemical dependency?
- **Anxiety**—Does the child worry about the situation at home?
- **Embarrassment**—Is the child ashamed to invite friends home or ask for help?
- **Distrustful**—Does the child have difficulty trusting others due to distrust of a parent?
- **Confusion**—Does the lack of a regular schedule at home or fluctuating temperaments of parents create instability?
- **Anger**—Is the child angry at the addicted parent or at the nonaddicted parent for enabling?
- **Depression**—Does the child feel lonely and helpless to change the situation?
- **Hypervigilant**—Is the child especially sensitive to the moods of others?
- **Overly responsible**—Is the child quick to assume responsibility for others?
- **People-pleaser**—Does the child avoid conflict at any cost?

“Jesus said to his disciples:
‘Things that cause people to sin
are bound to come, but woe to
that person through whom they come.
It would be better for him to be thrown
into the sea with a millstone tied
around his neck than for him to cause
one of these little ones to sin.’”
(Luke 17:1–2)

CAUSES FOR BEING CHEMICALLY DEPENDENT

Baseball great Mickey Mantle, who was both cheered and booed, once said, "Baseball didn't turn me into a drunk. I drank because I thought we were having fun. It was part of the camaraderie, the male bonding thing."[14]

While there can be numerous causes for a person's becoming an alcoholic, what could possibly contribute to the greatest switch hitter (one who batted both left-handed and right-handed) becoming addicted to alcohol? Mickey's father died of Hodgkin's disease at the young age of forty, and three other relatives succumbed to the same disease before their fortieth birthdays. For that reason, Mickey believed he also would die young, and the fear of dying gave him the impetus to "party hard" while he was young.

Mickey also remarked on the ready availability of alcohol in the sports world. Fans sent drinks to his table; hotel management sent complimentary bottles of wine to his room. Drinking helped fill the boredom of the frequent times of waiting, such as flying on planes and sitting around hotels. Mantle said, "In those days, how well you could hold your liquor was, for many of us, a measure of being a man."[15]

Little did Mantle know that his "measure of manhood" would poison his system and ultimately cause his death. Little did he know the caution given in the Word of God.

"Do not gaze at wine when it is red, when it sparkles in the cup, when it goes down smoothly! In the end it bites like a snake and poisons like a viper." (Proverbs 23:31–32)

HOW DOES a Chemical Dependency Develop?

People do not start their lives being dependent on substances, but they become dependent through repetition, by repeatedly using something to satisfy some need or longing.

While childhood sexual abuse and chronic bedwetting had been a part of his past, Mickey Mantle's addiction developed after the death of his father as he drank to help deal with depression, guilt, and fear.

Once drug use is established, a cycle develops that is common among those who abuse drugs. It is a vicious cycle that entraps and enslaves, but it is a cycle that can be broken!

Pain from the Past-Provocation

Past Pain

↓

Mood-altering drugs → Addiction → Violating values → Guilt → Shame → Mood-altering drugs

▶ **Mood-altering drugs**

"There is a way that seems right to a man, but in the end it leads to death." (Proverbs 14:12)

▶ **Addiction**

"When you were slaves to sin, you were free from the control of righteousness. What benefit did you reap at that time from the things you are now ashamed of? Those things result in death!" (Romans 6:20–21)

▶ **Violating values**

"Truthful lips endure forever, but a lying tongue lasts only a moment." (Proverbs 12:19)

▶ **Guilt**

"My guilt has overwhelmed me like a burden too heavy to bear." (Psalm 38:4)

- **Shame**

  "My disgrace is before me all day long, and my face is covered with shame." (Psalm 44:15)

"Even in laughter the heart may ache, and joy may end in grief." (Proverbs 14:13)

QUESTION: "How can I stop using drugs to escape the emotional pain of my past?

ANSWER: Face the fact of your painful past. Take steps to overcome making decisions motivated by your emotions and the need you feel to escape. As a child and as an unbeliever, you coped in ways that are now controlling you; those ways, however, are not true solutions. Emotions are responses to thinking. Therefore, if you are experiencing emotional pain ...

- ***Evaluate*** your painful thoughts and redirect them toward God.
- ***Pray*** for the people who come to mind, reaffirming your forgiveness of them and committing them to God.
- ***Verbalize*** to the Lord your commitment to reflect the character of Christ. He prayed for his enemies, and you have His Spirit within you, enabling you to forgive and to focus your thoughts on things that are uplifting for you and that encourage you in your walk with the Lord.

"When I was a child, I talked like a child, I thought like a child, I reasoned like a child. When I became a man, I put childish ways behind me. Now we see but a poor reflection as in a mirror; then we shall see face to face. Now I know in part; then I shall know fully, even as I am fully known."
(1 Corinthians 13:11–12)

QUESTION: "Is there any objective data apart from the Bible or cultural morality that supports a case against drinking alcohol?"

ANSWER: Yes, while numbers can change from year to year, the following statistics from 1993 taken within the United States prove to be quite sobering.[16]

- 25% of American families have problems because of alcohol.
- 33% of marriage failures are alcohol related.
- 25–40% of people receiving hospital treatment do so as a result of alcohol.
- 41% of all auto fatalities are alcohol related (U.S. Department of Transportation).[17]
- 50–67% of all murders and major assaults involve alcohol.

If you are trying to quit drinking, consider reading the following passage every day to strengthen your stand and to reinforce your resolve.

"Wine is a mocker and beer a brawler; whoever is led astray by them is not wise." (Proverbs 20:1)

QUESTION: "What could possibly discourage someone from smoking cigarettes or using other tobacco products?"[18]

ANSWER: Tobacco smoke contains more than 200 known poisons. Those who smoke two packs a day shorten their life expectancy by eight years.

Tobacco ...

- ▶ Is the most common cause of lung cancer
- ▶ Causes emphysema, making breathing very taxing, which in turn causes death
- ▶ Is a major cause of hardening of the arteries, which in turn causes strokes and ***most*** heart attacks
- ▶ Is a major contributor in mouth and throat cancers, which can disfigure a person for life
- ▶ Produces chemicals that erode the lining of the stomach, which in turn causes gastric ulcers
- ▶ Increases the risk of bladder cancer
- ▶ Produces carbon monoxide and retards the growth of a fetus in a mother who smokes, which also increases the risk of premature birth and infant death
- ▶ Contributes to heart disease, the leading cause of death for men

"'Everything is permissible'—but not everything is beneficial. 'Everything is permissible'—but everything is not constructive." (1 Corinthians 10:23)

WHAT ARE the Most Influential Factors?

No two people have exactly the same story about what contributed to their developing a drug dependency. But no matter how many factors are involved in becoming chemically dependent, they all fit into one of two categories: external or internal influences.

▶ **External Influences:** family and social

- ***Family environment***—Were you raised in a family that accepts social drinking?
- ***Dysfunctional family***—Have you used drugs to relieve emotional pain?
- ***Physical problems***—Are you dependent on medication for backaches, headaches, sleeplessness, dieting?
- ***Social acceptance***—Have you been served alcohol at most social functions?
- ***Peer pressure***—Are you seeking social acceptance by those who use drugs?
- ***Cultural endorsement***—Have you been continuously exposed to alcohol through TV, movies, advertisements, and magazines?

"Do not conform any longer to the pattern of this world, but be transformed by the renewing of your mind. Then you will be able to test and approve what God's will is—his good, pleasing and perfect will."
(Romans 12:2)

QUESTION: "Without offending them, how can I say *no* to my friends who drink heavily and offer me drinks?"

ANSWER: A simple "No thank you," or "Thank you, I'm not interested," should suffice. Most people do not like drinking or doing drugs alone, but most will also respect—if not envy—someone who is strong enough to not follow the crowd. If they are offended, that is a reflection on their own insecurity, not on your convictions.

You and you alone are accountable for the boundaries you set for your life. Anyone can give in to peer pressure, but only those who have strength of character will resist the pressure. Be aware that your enticers are walking on dangerous ground. The Bible says,

"Woe to him who gives drink to his neighbors, pouring it from the wineskin till they are drunk."
(Habakkuk 2:15)

▶ **Internal Influences**: genetic and psychological

- ***Inherited inclination from family***—Were you born to an alcoholic parent, or do you have close relatives who are alcoholics? (The risk for alcohol dependence is ***three to four times higher*** for those who have close relatives with a dependence on alcohol.[19])
- ***Inherited vulnerability from an ethnic group***—Were you born within an ethnic group that has a high rate of alcoholism? (Scandinavians, Northern Europeans, and the Irish are more susceptible, whereas Asians are less susceptible. "The low prevalence rates among Asians appear to relate to a deficiency, in perhaps 50% of Japanese, Chinese and Korean individuals, of the form of aldehyde dehydrogenase that eliminates low levels of the first breakdown product of alcohol, acetaldehyde."[20])

  Alcoholics process alcohol in a way that sustains and reinforces their addiction. Unlike nonalcoholics, it is difficult for them to process a chemical in alcohol metabolism called acetaldehyde, creating collateral addictive chemical compounds that interfere with the brain's process and create an opiate-like addiction.[21]
- ***Psychological makeup***—Are you prone to seek drugs as a relief from anxiety or stress? Alcohol soothes underlying nerves and thus calms the intense responses to stress

such as perspiring palms, skin flushing, and increased heart rate and blood pressure.

- ***Habits and compulsions***—Do you have habits that are resistant to change? (Repetitive actions alter the brain itself where connections between neurons are slowly modified, thus making it more difficult to make different choices.)

  No matter the reason for any enslaving habit that has mastery over us, God says we can change masters: "*A man is a slave to whatever has mastered him*" (2 Peter 2:19).

"Prepare your minds for action; be self-controlled." (1 Peter 1:13)

QUESTION: "Is alcoholism an inherited disease over which I have no control?"

ANSWER: Medical professionals continue to debate whether or not alcoholism is a disease. Because of the strong and lasting changes alcohol can have on the brain and other organs, many consider it a disease. Others take the position that it is more behavioral.

A disease is an abnormal condition of the body caused by ...[22]

▶ ***Infection*** (for example, catching the flu or smallpox from outside the body)

- ***Genetic defect*** (for example, being born with diabetes or with a genetic makeup where alcohol is not processed normally)
- ***Environmental factors*** (for example, being exposed to toxins and pollutants; developing cirrhosis of the liver where excessive alcohol has caused so much stress on the liver that it no longer functions properly)

While alcoholism can be influenced by genetics and by chemical alterations, the vital fact to remember is that you do have control over whether you succumb to alcoholism or whether you are restored from alcoholism. Your family background and genetics can make you more susceptible to alcoholism; however, these influences can be resisted. By preplanning to exercise self-control, you can set boundaries and protect yourself from problems with alcohol.

QUESTION: "What can I do to reduce my risk of becoming an alcoholic?"

ANSWER: Because the risk for alcoholism is higher among people who begin drinking at an early age, avoiding underage drinking reduces your risk.[23]

As an adult, the best way you can avoid alcoholism is to avoid drinking. However, if you drink in moderation, you reduce your risk by having no more than one drink a day if you are a woman or two drinks a day if you are a man.

If you have a family history of alcoholism, you should be especially careful even when considering moderate drinking. If you are a recovering alcoholic, a woman who is pregnant or is trying to become pregnant, or if you are engaged in activities that require attention or skill, you should not drink at all.[24]

"A prudent man sees danger and takes refuge, but the simple keep going and suffer for it." (Proverbs 22:3)

WHAT EXCUSES Do People Give?[25]

No one has to be taught the art of justifying behavior, but all of us manage to somehow learn it. People who are chemically dependent become proficient at rattling off reason after reason for using their drug of choice, but, ultimately, there is no valid justification, only excuses. In the final analysis, they are persuaded that they genuinely need it, or they feel entitled just because they want it.

▶ **"I need it ...**

- to pick me up."
- to quiet me down."
- to relieve my pain."
- to be more sociable."
- to forget my failures."
- to satisfy my cravings."

▶ **"I want it ...**

- to relax."
- to feel good."
- to have more fun."
- to relieve my stress."
- to be more accepted."
- to escape my situation."

"All a man's ways seem innocent to him, but motives are weighed by the LORD." (Proverbs 16:2)

QUESTION: "If alcoholism can be both inherited and a disease, how can it be a sin? Since I'm an alcoholic, isn't it beyond my control?"

ANSWER: It is not a sin for you to be a *nondrinking* alcoholic, but it is a sin for you to be a *drunk* alcoholic. Drunkenness is listed with other sins that we are commanded to avoid. While alcoholism may be a disease over which you have no control, drunkenness is clearly a sin over which you *do* have control. Choosing not to drink is setting a boundary for your life that will break the power of sin over you.

"Do not let sin reign in your mortal body so that you obey its evil desires." (Romans 6:12)

WHAT IS the Root Cause?

Initially people take drugs for two reasons: either to treat a legitimate medical problem or simply to feel a pleasurable sensation.

Those who are trying to feel different typically begin drinking or using other drugs because of peer pressure or to satisfy their curiosity. But they continue in order to satisfy their perceived needs. Substance abuse occurs when the substance moves from being a need-meeter to becoming the need itself. Instead of using a substance to relieve stress, the mere absence of the substance in the body causes stress.

God designed you with legitimate needs—physical, emotional, and spiritual—and a part of His design is for you to come to Him and to be dependent on Him to be your true Need-Meeter.

"My God will meet all your needs according to his glorious riches in Christ Jesus."
(Philippians 4:19)

▶ **Wrong Belief:**

"I don't have a chemical dependency. I just enjoy (alcohol and/or any other drug(s) of choice). I could stop at anytime, but drinking/using helps me cope with my difficult situations and eases my painful emotions."

▶ **Right Belief:**

"I realize that what I depend on in my life will have control of my life. I choose not to let any chemical have control over me. Instead, I choose to give Christ control of every area and to depend on Him to satisfy my needs." The Bible says, *"The Lord will guide you always; he will satisfy your needs in a sun-scorched land and will strengthen your frame. You will be like a well-watered garden, like a spring whose waters never fail"* (Isaiah 58:11).

Question: "How do I evaluate whether I should drink or not? I'm a new Christian and want to do what pleases God."

Answer: While the Bible does not prohibit the consumption of all alcohol, it does speak to the dangers of wine, beer, and strong alcoholic drinks. *"Wine is a mocker and beer a brawler"* (Proverbs 20:1). But for many people, the most persuasive argument for abstinence is "the stumbling argument": the concern that someone might stumble because of your questionable example. Since people tend to be followers, if you drink alcohol—or do drugs—those who follow your example could stumble, and their lives could be harmed because of following in your footsteps.

"It is better not to eat meat [sacrificed to idols] or drink wine or do anything else that will cause your brother to fall."
(Romans 14:21)

STEPS TO SOLUTION

To break free of an addiction, one must first recognize the problem and then be willing to face it and seek healing. For Mickey Mantle, an early wake-up call was the illness and subsequent death of his son, which resulted, in part, from a chemical dependency.

As Mickey agonized over the helplessness of watching his son die, then seeing the destruction of his family, he recognized that all four of his sons had a drinking problem and floundered as adults. Finally he realized that his approach to life wasn't working. Mickey admitted, "I couldn't go on the way I was living, drunk and sick and depressed, covering up with lies, trying to remember where I was going or where I had been."[26]

Despite his enormous fears of having to be open before others and to let others really know him, Mickey Mantle entered the Betty Ford Center and began the long, painful process of recovery. His son Mickey Jr. said, "Out of all the things he did, the World Series teams he starred on, the home runs he hit, the records he broke, his induction into the Hall of Fame, what I admired him for the most was getting sober."[27]

Mickey hit a home run in regard to his recovery. As he rounded the bases touching each of his three remaining sons—beginning a new relationship with each of them—he headed for "home" when he began treating his estranged wife differently. No more verbal abuse. No more emotional distancing. He found that he liked being sober, and he started telling his family he was proud of them. What a difference his changed life meant to his family and to himself! If only long ago he had known ...

"He who ignores discipline despises himself, but whoever heeds correction gains understanding." (Proverbs 15:32)

KEY VERSE TO MEMORIZE

"I am the Lord, your God, who takes hold of your right hand and says to you, Do not fear; I will help you." (Isaiah 41:13)

Key Passage to Read

1 Corinthians 10:12–33

Ten Truths about Temptation

#1 If you think you're standing firm, be careful that you don't fall. (v. 12)

#2 If you think your trial is unique, clearly it is not. (v. 13)

#3 God won't let you be tempted beyond what you can bear. (v. 13)

#4 God will provide a way for you to withstand the test. (v. 13)

#5 Everything is permissible—not everything is beneficial or constructive. (v. 23)

#6 Don't focus on yourself, but rather on the good of others. (v. 24)

#7 Don't violate the conscience of others; curb your freedom for their sake. (v. 29)

#8 Whatever you eat or drink, do it all for the glory of God. (v. 31)

#9 Do not cause anyone to stumble by your actions. (v. 32)

#10 Seek the good of others so that they might be truly saved. (v. 33)

QUESTION: "Does the Bible condemn drinking alcohol as sin?"

ANSWER: While the Bible does speak of medical benefits of wine (1 Timothy 5:23) and Jesus provided wine at a wedding (John 2:1–11), the Bible clearly condemns both *drunkenness* and *addiction* to alcohol as sinful.

God does not want you to lose control because of the influence of alcohol, but rather to yield to the controlling influence of the Holy Spirit. Addiction to alcohol or any other drug makes you a slave to that controlling substance. God wants you to be filled with the Holy Spirit and to be free.

"Do not get drunk on wine, which leads to debauchery. Instead, be filled with the Spirit." (Ephesians 5:18)

DELIVERANCE from Dependency[28]

Just as chemical dependency does not develop overnight, neither does deliverance from dependency occur overnight. There is a sequence of events that leads people into bondage and another sequence that leads people into freedom.

At the moment of your salvation, you were delivered from the penalty of sin (eternal death), and through the enablement of the indwelling Holy Spirit, you can experience being delivered from the power of destruction. But you must realize that freedom from the power of dependency is a process that requires focused, active participation on your part. You must choose to believe and practice the truth about yourself and God.

#1 **Admit you are powerless over your dependency.**

"I am unable to manage my life—I cannot control my life."

- ***Accept*** your dependent condition and your vulnerability to chemical addiction.
- ***Acknowledge*** your inability to manage your life and to overcome your drug dependency.
- ***Articulate*** to God your total inadequacy and your great need of His power in your life.

"Indeed, in our hearts we felt the sentence of death. But this happened that we might not rely on ourselves but on God, who raises the dead." (2 Corinthians 1:9)

#2 **Realize that the God who made you has the power to restore you.**

"I am asking Christ to be my Redeemer, to restore every area of my life."

- ***Accept*** the Lordship of Christ Jesus in your life as your Master, Ruler, and Owner.
- ***Acknowledge*** your need for God to comfort you and to restore you to wholeness.
- ***Articulate*** your gratitude to God for His saving power operating within your mind, will, and emotions, and thank Him for what He plans to do in and through your life.

"Though you have made me see troubles, many and bitter, you will restore my life again; from the depths of the earth you will again bring me up. You will increase my honor and comfort me once again." (Psalm 71:20–21)

#3 **Yield your will to the will of the Lord.**

"I am asking Christ to take control of my life."

- ***Accept*** the fact that your sinful nature died on the cross with Jesus and that sin (your addiction) is to no longer rule your life.

- ***Acknowledge*** the devastation that has resulted from your self-willed living in the past.
- ***Articulate*** your determination to stop your self-willed living and your decision to yield your will to the Lord.

"Jesus said to his disciples, 'If anyone would come after me, he must deny himself and take up his cross and follow me. For whoever wants to save his life will lose it, but whoever loses his life for me will find it.'" (Matthew 16:24–25)

#4 **Face reality—face your true self.**

"I will look honestly at my life, asking God to uncover my sins and character flaws."

- ***Accept*** the truth that you have deceived yourself about your chemical dependency and your desperate need for help.
- ***Acknowledge*** your reluctance in the past to face the truth about your sinful choices and patterns.
- ***Articulate*** to God and to others your willingness to know the truth about yourself and your commitment to honestly evaluate your life, your strengths, and your weaknesses.

"Search me, O God, and know my heart; test me and know my anxious thoughts. See if there is any offensive way in me, and lead me in the way everlasting." (Psalm 139:23–24)

#5 **Admit your struggle with sin, both to God and to someone else.**

"May I see my sin as God sees it and hate my sin as God hates it."

- ***Accept*** the depth and the duration of your struggle with chemical dependency.
- ***Acknowledge*** to a supportive person the power that the bondage to drugs has had over you, and confirm your present commitment to freedom.
- ***Articulate*** to both God and a friend your desire to overcome your chemical dependency and to live in the victory Jesus secured for you at Calvary.

"If we claim to be without sin, we deceive ourselves and the truth is not in us" (1 John 1:8)

#6 **Humbly accept God's help to change your patterns of the past.**

"I will commit my life into the care of Christ."

- ***Accept*** your limitations and your need for help in changing your unhealthy patterns of dealing with life.
- ***Acknowledge*** your frailty and the feebleness of your willpower and self-effort to effect change.
- ***Articulate*** to God your helplessness and your pledge to cooperate with Him as He changes you from the inside out.

"Humble yourselves, therefore, under God's mighty hand, that he may lift you up in due time. Cast all your anxiety on him because he cares for you." (1 Peter 5:6–7)

#7 **Confess your defects and daily failings.**

"I'm willing to see myself as God sees me."

- ***Accept*** that you are not perfect and that you will fail at times despite your good intentions.
- ***Acknowledge*** your failures immediately and confess them to God and to those you have offended. Then correct your course.
- ***Articulate*** any sins and shortcomings to God on a daily basis, and claim His forgiveness and cleansing.

"Create in me a pure heart, O God, and renew a steadfast spirit within me. Do not cast me from your presence or take your Holy Spirit from me. Restore to me the joy of your salvation and grant me a willing spirit, to sustain me." (Psalm 51:10–12)

#8 **Ask forgiveness of those offended.**

"I will find those whom I've hurt and from my heart ask forgiveness."

- ***Accept*** your need to ask forgiveness of anyone you offend, even though you may have been offended yourself.

- ***Acknowledge*** your great need of God's mercy and grace and your resolve to extend mercy and grace to others.
- ***Articulate*** to both God and to those you have offended your grief and regret and your resolve to change in the areas where you need to change.

"If you are offering your gift at the altar and there remember that your brother has something against you, leave your gift there in front of the altar. First go and be reconciled to your brother; then come and offer your gift." (Matthew 5:23–24)

#9 **Make restitution where you have wronged others.**

"I will make amends and go to do so with the help of God."

- ***Accept*** your obligation to do whatever is within your power in order to right your wrongs.
- ***Acknowledge*** to God and to those whom you have wronged your desire to make amends in any way possible.
- ***Articulate*** your responsibility to make restitution and your commitment to repay whatever debt you owe, whether it's money or labor, correcting a lie, showing respect, or extending love.

"If he gives back what he took in pledge for a loan, returns what he has stolen, follows the decrees that give life, and does no evil, he will surely live; he will not die. None of the sins he has committed will be remembered against him. He has done what is just and right; he will surely live." (Ezekiel 33:15–16)

#10 **Keep a clean slate when you realize you have been wrong.**

"Each day I will take responsibility for my irresponsibility."

- ***Accept*** your charge to keep a clean slate before God and every person.
- ***Acknowledge*** each and every failure in order to live as God would have you to live.
- ***Articulate*** each failure to God on a moment by moment basis, making no excuses, but recommit to living a self-controlled, Spirit-empowered life.

"The grace of God that brings salvation has appeared to all men. It teaches us to say 'No' to ungodliness and worldly passions, and to live self-controlled, upright and godly lives." (Titus 2:11–12)

#11 Pray and know God's path for your life.

"I want to be led by the Lord and to be put only on His path."

- ***Accept*** your new dependence on God and your vital need to communicate with Him through Bible study and prayer.
- ***Acknowledge*** your need to have the prayer support of others to know God's truths and God's ways.
- ***Articulate*** to God your desire to be what He wants you to be and to do what He leads you to do.

"Show me your ways, O Lord, teach me your paths; guide me in your truth and teach me, for you are God my Savior, and my hope is in you all day long." (Psalm 25:4–5)

#12 Reach out to others with your hand and your heart.

"I will care for those who need care and will help with a heart of compassion."

- ***Accept*** your need of others and their need of you.
- ***Acknowledge*** your giftedness from God and His mandate to use your God-given gifts to serve others in tangible, practical ways.

- ***Articulate*** ways God may be leading you to minister to others and ask for His confirmation and for the guidance of mature Christians who can help you to reach out to others.

"Carry each other's burdens, and in this way you will fulfill the law of Christ." (Galatians 6:2)

PRAYER OF SALVATION

"God, I need You in my life.
I admit that I have sinned, and You have said that my sin deserves death.
Many times I've gone my own way instead of Your way.
Please forgive me for all of my sins.
Thank You, Jesus, for dying on the cross to pay the penalty for my sins.
Come into my life to be my Lord and Savior.
Take control of my life and make me the person You want me to be.
Thank You, Jesus, for what You will do in me, to me, and through me.
In Your holy name I pray. Amen."

QUESTION: "Since I became a new creation when I became a Christian, didn't that change my addictions and my tendency to sin?"

ANSWER: When you put your trust in Christ, you did indeed receive a new life! God's Spirit lives within you and is a new power source to enable you to overcome sin. While you have been saved from the penalty of sin (eternal separation from God) and while the power of sin over you has been broken, you must still choose not to sin when you are tempted. You must choose daily to put off your *old self* and refuse to be controlled by it. (Doing that includes the choice to put off your addictions and your addictive tendencies.) Then you must choose to put on your *new self* and to be controlled by it—that new self which was created to be like Christ.

"You were taught, with regard to your former way of life, to put off your old self, which is being corrupted by its deceitful desires; to be made new in the attitude of your minds; and to put on the new self, created to be like God in true righteousness and holiness." (Ephesians 4:22–24)

SEVEN DON'TS for Deliverance[29]

As you go through the process of deliverance from dependency, knowing what *not* to do can be just as helpful as knowing what *to* do.

#1 ***Don't*** fight addiction on your own. Participate in a legitimate drug recovery program.

"Two are better than one, because they have a good return for their work: If one falls down, his friend can help him up. But pity the man who falls and has no one to help him up!" (Ecclesiastes 4:9–10)

#2 ***Don't*** be blind about your ability to lie to yourself and to others!

"The heart is deceitful above all things and beyond cure. Who can understand it?" (Jeremiah 17:9)

#3 ***Don't*** socialize with those who encourage your habit.

"Do not be misled: 'Bad company corrupts good character.'" (1 Corinthians 15:33)

#4 ***Don't*** worry about the future. Walk with God one day at a time.

"Do not worry about tomorrow, for tomorrow will worry about itself. Each day has enough trouble of its own." (Matthew 6:34)

#5 ***Don't*** give up if you relapse. It is never too late for you to get back on track.

"If we confess our sins, he is faithful and just and will forgive us our sins and purify us from all unrighteousness." (1 John 1:9)

#6 **Don't** become prideful as you succeed in the recovery process.

"Pride goes before destruction, a haughty spirit before a fall." (Proverbs 16:18)

#7 **Don't** be surprised at temptation!

"No temptation has seized you except what is common to man. And God is faithful; he will not let you be tempted beyond what you can bear. But when you are tempted, he will also provide a way out so that you can stand up under it." (1 Corinthians 10:13)

QUESTION: "When I became a Christian a year ago, I kicked cocaine and marijuana for eight months. But now I'm back on marijuana with no *motivation to quit*. How can I overcome this habit?"

ANSWER: Motivation is a vital factor in overcoming any addiction. The more you realize that you are not only causing great harm to yourself, but also grieving the heart of God, the more you will have "good guilt," which can produce the motivation you lack. The Bible says we are changed by the renewing of our minds, which is another key to overcoming a destructive habit. You previously relied on the power of Christ within you, but along the way your focus changed, and you left your power source. Rather than focusing on what you should do, focus on being conformed to the character of Christ. Repent from doing what merely pleases you, and do the things you did when you were first saved.

"I hold this against you: You have forsaken your first love [Jesus]. Remember the height from which you have fallen! Repent and do the things you did at first."
(Revelation 2:4–5)

TEN SPIRITUAL Tips for Recovery[30]

Your freedom must first be gained in the spiritual realm before it can be experienced in the physical and emotional realms. Take to heart the following tips as you walk down the road to recovery.

#1 The ***time to begin*** your recovery is today.

"Today, if you hear his voice, do not harden your hearts as you did in the rebellion." (Hebrews 3:15)

#2 ***Realize*** that recovery is a lifelong process, not a onetime event.

"Not that I have already obtained all this, or have already been made perfect, but I press on to take hold of that for which Christ Jesus took hold of me." (Philippians 3:12)

#3 ***Pray daily*** for victory! It is through prayer that God protects you.

"Watch and pray so that you will not fall into temptation. The spirit is willing, but the body is weak." (Matthew 26:41)

#4 ***Read your Bible*** every day in order to get strength from God.

"My soul is weary with sorrow; strengthen me according to your word." (Psalm 119:28)

#5 ***Meditate on Scripture*** to fight against falling into sin.

"I have hidden your word in my heart that I might not sin against you." (Psalm 119:11)

#6 ***Attend church*** every week to worship God and to grow with others.

"Let us consider how we may spur one another on toward love and good deeds. Let us not give up meeting together, as some are in the habit of doing, but let us encourage one another." (Hebrews 10:24–25)

#7 ***Share your struggles*** with caring loved ones.

"Confess your sins to each other and pray for each other so that you may be healed." (James 5:16)

#8 ***Have confidence in God!*** Prioritize growing in your relationship with Him.

"Seek first his kingdom and his righteousness, and all these things will be given to you as well." (Matthew 6:33)

#9 ***Depend on Christ's strength*** to stay drug free.

"I can do everything through him who gives me strength." (Philippians 4:13)

#10 ***Know*** that permanent ***change is possible.***

"Nothing is impossible with God." (Luke 1:37)

QUESTION: "I am a recovering addict but I've continued to relapse. Recently, I've become a Christian, and now I feel that God has delivered me. Is that possible?"

ANSWER: Some Christians do receive a supernatural deliverance from drugs, while others do not. No matter which is true in your case, by accepting Jesus Christ as your personal Lord and Savior, there is good news for you. When you received authentic salvation, you not only were saved from the *penalty of sin*, but were also saved from the *power of sin*. Drugs are no longer your master—Jesus is now your Master. Through the power of Christ living in you, you can rely on His supernatural power for deliverance over your addiction.

"We know that our old self was crucified with him so that the body of sin might be done away with, that we should no longer be slaves to sin. ... For sin shall not be your master, because you are not under the law, but under grace." (Romans 6:6, 14)

SET BENEFICIAL Boundaries with the One Addicted

Boundaries are barriers that protect from external harm and guard against internal harm. Those involved with someone struggling with a chemical dependency need to learn how to set appropriate limits on what they do for their loved one. These boundaries will help prevent you from taking on excessive responsibilities that belong to your loved one. Boundaries serve to keep the *addict's* problem from becoming *your* problem.

"Above all else, guard your heart, for it is the wellspring of life." (Proverbs 4:23)

▶ Give up all expectations of the addict.

"Find rest, O my soul, in God alone; my hope comes from him." (Psalm 62:5)

▶ Learn to detach from the addict's problem, and take control of your life.

"My eyes are ever on the Lord, for only he will release my feet from the snare." (Psalm 25:15)

▶ Shift your focus from the addict's behavior to your responses.

"Let us examine our ways and test them, and let us return to the Lord." (Lamentations 3:40)

- Learn all you can about drug abuse.

  "How much better to get wisdom than gold, to choose understanding rather than silver!" (Proverbs 16:16)

- Stop acts that are enabling (making excuses, protecting).

  "These things you have done and I kept silent; you thought I was altogether like you. But I will rebuke you and accuse you to your face." (Psalm 50:21)

- Let the addict know the effects the addiction has had on you and on others.

  "Each of you must put off falsehood and speak truthfully to his neighbor, for we are all members of one body." (Ephesians 4:25)

- Pray for and expect God to bring consequences into the addict's life.

  "A man's ways are in full view of the Lord, *and he examines all his paths. The evil deeds of a wicked man ensnare him; the cords of his sin hold him fast. He will die for lack of discipline, led astray by his own great folly."* (Proverbs 5:21–23)

QUESTION: "When my *husband drinks* too much, he gets angry and *physically abusive.* What should I do to protect myself and my children and still remain biblically submissive to my husband?"

ANSWER: The Bible never says that a wife—in the name of submission—is to submit to domestic violence. A husband's substance abuse never gives him the right to dole out physical abuse. Conversely, the Bible says, *"Do not associate with one easily angered"* (Proverbs 22:24). Therefore, communicate your boundaries. Tell him that if he is abusive again, you will call the police. He can no longer live at home. You will leave with the children. Then follow through if he again violates the boundary.

> **"A hot-tempered man must pay the penalty; if you rescue him, you will have to do it again."**
> **(Proverbs 19:19)**

CONDUCT a Crisis Intervention with the One Addicted[31]

Most often, the most powerful act on behalf of a substance abuser is a *crisis intervention*—it is effective 80 percent of the time. And the most powerful aspect of a crisis intervention is the group dynamic—*there is power in numbers!* Typically a family member will seek to stop the addict's behavior, but sadly the appeal falls on deaf ears. In privacy, others state their concern, but one by one each plea is dismissed. As individuals they are powerless—as a group they are dynamite. In fact, a group can be empowered by God to move the immovable. God's Word lays out the blueprint for such an intervention.

"If your brother sins against you, go and show him his fault, just between the two of you. If he listens to you, you have won your brother over. But if he will not listen, take one or two others along, so that 'every matter may be established by the testimony of two or three witnesses.'"
(Matthew 18:15–16)
(See also Ezekiel 3:18–19.)

- Pray for wisdom and understanding from the Lord.

  "The Lord *gives wisdom, and from his mouth come knowledge and understanding."* (Proverbs 2:6)

- Educate yourself regarding crisis intervention programs. Attend meetings on chemical dependency (for example, Overcomers Outreach, Alcoholics Anonymous, Al-Anon, and Narcotics Anonymous). Read materials on intervention and visit treatment facilities.

  "Blessed is the man who finds wisdom, the man who gains understanding, for she [wisdom] is more profitable than silver and yields better returns than gold." (Proverbs 3:13–14)

- Call a counseling office to refer you to a Christian leader trained in intervention procedures.

  "Plans fail for lack of counsel, but with many advisers they succeed." (Proverbs 15:22)

- If possible, meet with an intervention specialist to plan the approach. Discussion needs to include treatment program options, preadmission plans, procedures, insurance, and the impact of treatment on the addict's employment.

  "Listen to advice and accept instruction, and in the end you will be wise." (Proverbs 19:20)

- Enlist the aid of key people who have been affected by the addict's harmful behavior and are willing to confront (caring family, friends, doctor, employer, coworkers, and spiritual leader).

  "A truthful witness saves lives." (Proverbs 14:25)

- In absolute confidentiality and *without the addict present*, hold a first meeting in which these key people rehearse (if possible with the trained leader) what they will say, how they will say it, and the order in which they will speak when confronting.

  "Better is open rebuke than hidden love. Wounds from a friend can be trusted." (Proverbs 27:5–6)

- Hold a second meeting *with the addict present* where one at a time each key confronter communicates genuine care for the addict and shares the rehearsed confrontations (The Four *P*s of an Appeal).

  "Reckless words pierce like a sword, but the tongue of the wise brings healing." (Proverbs 12:18)

The Four *Ps* of an Appeal[32]

#1 **The Personal**

▶ Affirm rather than attack.

"I want you to know how much I care about you (or love you), and I am terribly concerned about you."

"Do not let any unwholesome talk come out of your mouths, but only what is helpful for building others up according to their needs, that it may benefit those who listen." (Ephesians 4:29)

#2 **The Past**

▶ Give a recent, specific example describing the addict's negative behavior and the personal impact it had on you.

"Last night when you slurred your speech in front of my friend, I was humiliated."

"A truthful witness gives honest testimony." (Proverbs 12:17)

▶ Be brief, keeping examples to three or four sentences.

"A man of knowledge uses words with restraint, and a man of understanding is even-tempered." (Proverbs 17:27)

#3 The Pain

- Emphasize the painful impact the addict's behavior has had on you. Use "I" statements.

  "I was devastated and deeply hurt because of the way you yelled at me."

  "A wise man's heart guides his mouth, and his lips promote instruction." (Proverbs 16:23)

#4 The Plea

- Make a personal plea for your loved one to receive treatment.

  "I plead with you to get the help you need to overcome your addiction. If you are willing, you will have my deepest respect."

  "The tongue has the power of life and death." (Proverbs 18:21)

- Be prepared to implement an immediate plan if treatment is agreed on.

  "Your bags have been packed, and you have been accepted into the treatment program at ______________________."

  "Rescue those being led away to death; hold back those staggering toward slaughter. If you say, 'But we knew nothing about this,' does not he who weighs the heart perceive it? Does not he who guards your life know it? Will he not repay each person according to what he has done?" (Proverbs 24:11–12)

- If treatment is refused, detail the repercussions.

  "We cannot allow you to come home or to be with our family until you have been clean and sober for (name a specific period of time)."

  "Stern discipline awaits him who leaves the path; he who hates correction will die." (Proverbs 15:10)

The Don'ts of Dialogue[33]

We can be on the side of *right*, yet our actions can be *wrong*. Many times we can influence a person to want to change, not by what we say but by how we say it. The Word of God says, *"If someone is caught in a sin, you who are spiritual should restore him gently"* (Galatians 6:1).

- ***Don't*** involve yourself in name-calling, preaching, or being judgmental.

  "Last night you were a jerk. Who wants to be with a drunk?"

  "A man who lacks judgment derides his neighbor, but a man of understanding holds his tongue." (Proverbs 11:12)

- ***Don't*** come to the defense of the addict when others are confronting.

  "He really didn't mean to hurt you."

  "There is a ... time to be silent and a time to speak." (Ecclesiastes 3:1, 7)

▶ ***Don't*** argue if your facts are disputed.

"You may be right, but what I've read is different."

"The Lord's servant must not quarrel. ... Those who oppose him he must gently instruct, in the hope that God will grant them repentance leading them to a knowledge of the truth, and that they will come to their senses and escape from the trap of the devil, who has taken them captive to do his will." (2 Timothy 2:24–26)

▶ ***Don't*** over react—keep your emotions under control.

If verbally attacked, calmly state your position, and if again opposed, calmly repeat the same words again ... and again. "This is in your best interest."

"Everyone should be quick to listen, slow to speak and slow to become angry, for man's anger does not bring about the righteous life that God desires." (James 1:19–20)

▶ ***Don't*** give ultimatums unless you are prepared to follow through with them.

If your loved one, who has been away for only a short time, says, "I promise not to do it anymore; just let me come back this one time," you say, "No, you cannot come back until you have completed treatment."

"Let your 'Yes' be yes, and your 'No,' no." (James 5:12)

- ***Don't*** shield your loved one from facing the consequences of addiction.

  "I will not lie to your boss again."

  "A man reaps what he sows." (Galatians 6:7)

- ***Don't*** accept promises with no commitment for immediate action.

  "I can't go now, but I promise to go next month."

  "A simple man believes anything, but a prudent man gives thought to his steps." (Proverbs 14:15)

This second meeting concludes with the addict either immediately entering a treatment program or experiencing the consequences of refusing treatment.

"He who rebukes a man will in the end gain more favor than he who has a flattering tongue." (Proverbs 28:23)

QUESTION: "What can I do to help my grandchildren whose parents are both alcoholics and are violent and combative when intoxicated?"

ANSWER: Several options could be considered:

- Calls to crisis intervention could be made by several significant people.
- Report the situation to a local CPS office (Child Protective Services).
- Report drunk and disorderly conduct to the local police department.
- Petition the court for custody of minor children.

Prayerfully consider which option would hold the greatest possibility for effecting change, and, with the support of prayer partners, develop a plan. Consult with a professional in this area, if possible.

"Plans fail for lack of counsel,
but with many advisers they succeed."
(Proverbs 15:22)

REALIZE THE Power of Prayer on Behalf of the One Addicted

Prayer is accessing God. Prayer is bringing all that He is into this situation. Through prayer, ask that His power and peace be your power and peace.

"His divine power has given us everything we need for life and godliness through our knowledge of him who called us by his own glory and goodness. Through these he has given us his very great and precious promises, so that through them you may participate in the divine nature and escape the corruption in the world caused by evil desires." (2 Peter 1:3–4)

- Pray with thanksgiving for what God has done for you.

  "Do not be anxious about anything, but in everything, by prayer and petition, with thanksgiving, present your requests to God. And the peace of God, which transcends all understanding, will guard your hearts and your minds in Christ Jesus." (Philippians 4:6–7)

- Pray for God to reveal your harmful responses.

  "Surely you desire truth in the inner parts; you teach me wisdom in the inmost place." (Psalm 51:6)

- Pray for more love for the offender.

  "My command is this: Love each other as I have loved you." (John 15:12)

- Pray for strongholds to be broken.

  "The weapons we fight with are not the weapons of the world. On the contrary, they have divine power to demolish strongholds. We demolish arguments and every pretension that sets itself up against the knowledge of God, and we take captive every thought to make it obedient to Christ." (2 Corinthians 10:4–5)

- Pray for faith that, with God, lasting change is possible.

  "All things are possible with God." (Mark 10:27)

- Pray for the addicted person.

  "For this reason, since the day we heard about you, we have not stopped praying for you and asking God to fill you with the knowledge of his will through all spiritual wisdom and understanding. And we pray this in order that you may live a life worthy of the Lord and may please him in every way: bearing fruit in every good work, growing in the knowledge of God, being strengthened with all power according to his glorious might so that you may have great endurance and patience." (Colossians 1:9–11)

- Pray with consistence and persistence.

  "Pray continually." (1 Thessalonians 5:17)

"Enter his gates with thanksgiving and his courts with praise; give thanks to him and praise his name. For the Lord is good and his love endures forever; his faithfulness continues through all generations." (Psalm 100:4–5)

QUESTION: "Should I continue to be around my alcoholic father again and again when he is abusive to me?"

ANSWER: Would you continue to put your hand in a fire again and again when you know it will burn you? Obviously not. You would maintain a healthy distance. Likewise, you need to establish not only a healthy physical distance from your father, but an emotional distance as well. That is why you need to present a "boundary" to your father. When your father is not being abusive, explain that you love him and want to see him, but that his verbal abuse is too painful for you to be around. Therefore, you are setting a boundary. Simply put, if he becomes abusive, you will quietly, but quickly, leave his presence. Be aware that he will test you to see whether you will actually leave. Emphasize that the choice is up to him! If, instead, he wants to spend time with you, he will have to choose to stop being abusive. Be sure to follow through with what you've told him. Quickly leave every time he begins to be abusive. In time he will see that you mean what you say. Ultimately, he will respect you and hopefully will begin to think before he speaks.

"There is ... a time to embrace and a time to refrain." (Ecclesiastes 3:1, 5)

It Is Never Too Late

Mickey Mantle's story was one of success as he gained control over the unmanageability of his life. But there was still something missing.[34]

When Mickey was diagnosed with liver cancer, he knew he was facing death. He called his longtime friend and former teammate, second baseman Bobby Richardson. Knowing that Bobby was a committed Christian, Mickey asked him to pray for him over the telephone. As the cancer progressed to an even more critical stage, Mickey's death seemed imminent, and the family once again called Bobby Richardson. As he entered Mantle's hospital room, Bobby remembered the many times he had talked to Mickey about the Lord and once again made the appeal, "Mickey, I love you, and I want you to spend eternity in heaven with me." Mantle smiled and said, "Bobby, I've been wanting to tell you that I have trusted Jesus Christ as my Savior."[35]

At Mickey's funeral, Bobby Richardson told the audience that there are only two kinds of people: those who say "yes" to Christ and those who say "no." And since none of us knows how much time we still have on earth, saying "maybe" is really the same as saying "no."

Before Mickey's death, he made this poignant statement: "It's hard to look back. But you learn from it. ... I want to make a difference, not because I hit home runs, but because I changed my life. If I can, anyone can. It is never too late."[36]

If you have never seriously considered where you would spend eternity or if you have always thought you had plenty of time to decide, make today the day of decision. Just as Mickey Mantle realized near the end of his life that he needed to be forgiven of his sins, you may feel the Lord leading you to the same conclusion. If your desire is to live in a right relationship with the Lord, you can pray for Him to enter your heart and take control of your life, no matter how unmanageable it may have become.

"Teach me to do your will,
for you are my God; may your good Spirit
lead me on level ground."
(Psalm 143:10)

Don't Give Up Hope!

Bobby Richardson never gave up on Mickey Mantle. How blessed was the Mick to have a faithful friend who consistently shared Christ with him. Bobby represented the heart of these two verses.

"My brothers, if one of you should wander from the truth and someone should bring him back, remember this: Whoever turns a sinner from the error of his way will save him from death and cover over a multitude of sins." (James 5:19–20)

Bobby knew that in the last inning of his life, Mickey had passed over from death to life because Jesus said ...

"I tell you the truth, whoever hears my word and believes him who sent me has eternal life and will not be condemned; he has crossed over from death to life." (John 5:24)

SCRIPTURES TO MEMORIZE

Why is it important for me to talk about my drug problem when I feel embarrassed to ask for **advice** or **accept instruction**?

> *"Listen to* ***advice*** *and* ***accept instruction****, and in the end you will be wise."* (Proverbs 19:20)

Does God expect me to keep on suffering abuse, or is it all right to **take refuge**?

> *"A prudent man sees danger and* ***takes refuge****, but the simple keep going and suffer for it."* (Proverbs 22:3)

Is it **unwise** to think I can handle my drug problem alone? Am I being **led astray**?

> *"Wine is a mocker and beer a brawler; whoever is* ***led astray*** *by them is* ***not wise****."* (Proverbs 20:1)

Why shouldn't I **gaze at** and taste the **sparkle of wine** when it looks so appealing?

> *"Do not* ***gaze at wine*** *when it is red, when it* ***sparkles*** *in the cup, when it goes down smoothly! In the end it bites like a snake and poisons like a viper."* (Proverbs 23:31–32)

Is it possible for me to **please God** and still follow the **pattern of the world**?

> *"In view of God's mercy ... offer your bodies as living sacrifices, holy and* ***pleasing to God****—this is your spiritual act of worship. Do not conform any longer to the* ***pattern of this world****, but be transformed by the renewing of your mind. Then you will be able to test and approve what God's will is—his good, pleasing and perfect will."* (Romans 12:1–2)

I know my body is **God's temple**, but don't I have the right to do with it as I please without fearing that **God will destroy** me?

> *"Don't you know that you yourselves are* ***God's temple*** *and that God's Spirit lives in you? If anyone destroys God's temple,* ***God will destroy*** *him; for God's temple is sacred, and you are that temple."* (1 Corinthians 3:16–17)

What harm is there in **drinking wine** or using any drugs in the presence of others when it is socially acceptable?

> *"It is better not to eat meat or* ***drink wine*** *or to do anything else that will cause your brother to fall."* (Romans 14:21)

How is it **possible** to break the hold of my addiction when it has controlled my life for years?

> *"All things are* ***possible*** *with God."* (Mark 10:27)

What can I do to be **released** from the **snare** of my addiction?

> *"My eyes are ever on the* Lord, *for only he will* ***release*** *my feet from the* ***snare****."* (Psalm 25:15)

Can I ever hope to find **a way out** of a **temptation that is beyond what I can bear** and **stand up under**?

> *"No* ***temptation*** *has seized you except what is common to man. And God is faithful; he will not let you be tempted* ***beyond what you can bear****. But when you are tempted, he will also provide* ***a way out*** *so that you can* ***stand up under it****."* (1 Corinthians 10:13)

NOTES

1. Merlyn Mantle, et al., with Mickey Herskowitz, *A Hero All His Life: A Memoir by the Mantle Family* (New York: HarperCollins, 1996); Ed Cheek, *Mickey Mantle: His Final Inning* (Garland, TX: ATS, n.d.).
2. Mantle, et al., *Hero All His Life*, 34.
3. Stephen Van Cleave, Walter Byrd, and Kathy Revell, *Counseling for Substance Abuse and Addiction*, edited by Gary R. Collins, Resources for Christian Counseling, vol. 12 (Dallas: Word, 1987), 36, 181.
4. James R. Beck, "Substance-Use Disorders," in *Baker Encyclopedia of Psychology*, ed. David G. Benner (Grand Rapids: Baker, 1985), 1128–29.
5. Jeff VanVonderen, *Good News for the Chemically Dependent and Those Who Love Them*, rev. and updated ed. (Nashville: Thomas Nelson, 1991), 21–22.
6. American Psychiatric Association, *Diagnostic and Statistical Manual of Mental Disorders*, 4th ed., text revision (Washington, DC: American Psychiatric Association, 2000), 191–209.
7. Elizabeth J. Taylor, ed., *Dorland's Illustrated Medical Dictionary*, 27th ed. (Philadelphia, PA: W. B. Saunders, 1988), 848.
8. Collette Shaughnessy, *Reachout*, Q & A Columns, March 1999, Lowe Family Foundation, http://www.lowefamily.org/reachout/mar99.html; Van Cleave, Byrd, and Revell, *Counseling for Substance Abuse and Addiction*, 94–95, 181.
9. Mantle, et al., *Hero All His Life*, 98.
10. Mantle, et al., *Hero All His Life*, 19.
11. Substance Abuse and Mental Health Services Administration, "Summary of Findings from the 2000 National Household Survey on Drug Abuse (NHSDA Series: H-13, DHHS Publication No. SMA 01-3549)," 2001, U.S. Department of Health and Human Services, http://www.samhsa.gov/oas/2k2/suicide/suicide.pdf.

12. Ronald Rogers and Chandler Scott McMillin, *Under Your Own Power: A Guide to Recovery for Nonbelievers .... and the Ones Who Love Them* (New York: G. P. Putnam's Sons, 1992), 140–43.

13. George R. Ross, *Treating Adolescent Substance Abuse: Understanding the Fundamental Elements* (Boston: Allyn and Bacon, 1993), 23–25; Andre Bustanoby, *When Your Child Is on Drugs or Alcohol* (San Bernardino, CA: Here's Hope, 1986), 17–18.

14. Mantle, et al., *Hero All His Life*, 16.

15. Mantle, et al., *Hero All His Life*, 5.

16. Institute for Health Policy, Brandeis University, "Substance Abuse: The Nation's Number One Health Problem; Key Indicators for Policy," October 1993, The Robert Wood Johnson Foundation, http://said.dol.gov/htree13.

17. U.S. Department of Transportation, National Highway Traffic Safety Administration, "Traffic Safety Facts 2001: A Compilation of Motor Vehicle Crash Data from the Fatality Analysis Reporting System and the General Estimates System," 2001, http://www-nrd.nhtsa.dot.gov/pdf/nrd-30/NCSA/TSFAnn/TSF2001.pdf.

18. *The World's Best Anatomical Charts: Diseases and Disorders* (Skokie, IL: Anatomical Chart Company, 2000), 29.

19. American Psychiatric Association, *DSM-IV TR*, 221.

20. American Psychiatric Association, *DSM-IV TR*, 219.

21. Jarmes R. Milam and Katherine Ketcham, *Under the Influence* (New York: Bantam, 1983), 34–37. Quoted in Bustanoby, *When Your Child Is on Drugs or Alcohol*, 19.

22. *American Heritage Electronic Dictionary*, s.v. "Disease" (Houghton Mifflin, 1992).

23. Glen R. Hanson, "New Vista in Drug Abuse Prevention," n.d., 17 September 2003.

24. *A Family History of Alcoholism: Are You at Risk?* (Washington, D.C.: U.S. Department of Health and Human Services, 2003).

25. VanVonderen, *Good News for the Chemically Dependent and Those Who Love Them*, 31–32.

26. Mantle, et al., *Hero All His Life*, 26.

27. Mantle, et al., *Hero All His Life*, 153.

28. Robert S. McGee, Pat Springle, and Susan Joiner, *Rapha's Twelve-Step Program for Overcoming Chemical Dependency: with Support Materials from The Search for Significance.*, 2nd ed. (Houston, TX: Rapha, 1990); Van Cleave, Byrd, and Revell, *Counseling for Substance Abuse and Addiction*, 103–10.

29. Van Cleave, Byrd, and Revell, *Counseling for Substance Abuse and Addiction*, 116–17.

30. Van Cleave, Byrd, and Revell, *Counseling for Substance Abuse and Addiction*, 116–17.

31. Van Cleave, Byrd, and Revell, *Counseling for Substance Abuse and Addiction*, 83–6; Carolyn Johnson, *Understanding Alcoholism* (Grand Rapids: Zondervan, 1991), 145–50; Christina B. Parker, *When Someone You Love Drinks Too Much: A Christian Guide to Addiction, Codependence, & Recovery* (New York: Harper & Row, 1990), 55–56.

32. Van Cleave, Byrd, and Revell, *Counseling for Substance Abuse and Addiction*, 87.

33. Van Cleave, Byrd, and Revell, *Counseling for Substance Abuse and Addiction*, 86–87; Parker, *When Someone You Love Drinks Too Much*, 54–55.

34. Cheek, *Mickey Mantle.*

35. Cheek, *Mickey Mantle.*

36. Mantle, et al., *Hero All His Life*, 8.

SELECTED BIBLIOGRAPHY

American Psychiatric Association. *Diagnostic and Statistical Manual of Mental Disorders.* 4th ed., text revision. Washington, DC: American Psychiatric Association, 2000.

Beck, James R. "Substance-Use Disorders." In *Baker Encyclopedia of Psychology*, edited by David G. Benner, 1128–30. Grand Rapids: Baker, 1985.

Bustanoby, Andre. *When Your Child Is on Drugs or Alcohol.* San Bernardino, CA: Here's Hope, 1986.

Cheek, Ed. *Mickey Mantle: His Final Inning.* Garland, TX: ATS, n.d.

Crabb, Lawrence J., Jr. *Understanding People: Deep Longings for Relationship.* Ministry Resources Library. Grand Rapids: Zondervan, 1987.

Hunt, June. *Counseling Through Your Bible Handbook.* Eugene, Oregon: Harvest House Publishers, 2007.

Hunt, June. *How to Forgive ... When You Don't Feel Like It.* Eugene, Oregon: Harvest House Publishers, 2007.

Hunt, June. *How to Handle Your Emotions.* Eugene, Oregon: Harvest House Publishers, 2008.

Hunt, June. *Seeing Yourself Through God's Eyes.* Eugene, Oregon: Harvest House Publishers, 2008

Institute for Health Policy, Brandeis University. "Substance Abuse: The Nation's Number One Health Problem; Key Indicators for Policy." October 1993. The Robert Wood Johnson Foundation. http://said.dol.gov/htree13.

Johnson, Carolyn. *Understanding Alcoholism.* Grand Rapids: Zondervan, 1991.

Johnson, Jay, Jane Carlisle Maxwell, and Marian Leitnerschmidt. *A Dictionary of Slang Drug Terms, Trade Names, and Pharmacological Effects and Uses* (Austin, TX: Texas Commission on Alcohol and Drug Abuse, 1997), http://www.tcada.state.tx.us/research/slang/terms.pdf.

Mantle, Merlyn, et al., with Mickey Herskowitz. *A Hero All His Life: A Memoir by the Mantle Family.* New York: HarperCollins, 1996.

McGee, Robert S. *The Search for Significance.* 2nd ed. Houston, TX: Rapha, 1990.

McGee, Robert S., Pat Springle, and Susan Joiner. *Rapha's Twelve-Step Program for Overcoming Chemical Dependency: with Support Materials from The Search for Significance.* 2nd ed. Houston, TX: Rapha, 1990.

Milam, James R., and Katherine Ketcham. *Under the Influence.* New York: Bantam, 1983.

National Institute on Drug Abuse. "Commonly Abused Drugs" (Washington, D.C.: NIDA, n.d.), http://www.drugabuse.gov/DrugPages/DrugsofAbuse.html.

Parker, Christina B. *When Someone You Love Drinks Too Much: A Christian Guide to Addiction, Codependence, & Recovery*. New York: Harper & Row, 1990.

Rogers, Ronald, and Chandler Scott McMillin. *Under Your Own Power: A Guide to Recovery for Nonbelievers ... and the Ones Who Love Them*. New York: G. P. Putnam's Sons, 1992.

Ross, George R. *Treating Adolescent Substance Abuse: Understanding the Fundamental Elements*. Boston: Allyn and Bacon, 1993.

Shaughnessy, Collette. *Reachout. Q & A Columns*. March 1999. Lowe Family Foundation. http://www.lowefamily.org/reachout/mar99.html (accessed October 22, 2003).

Substance Abuse and Mental Health Services Administration. "Summary of Findings from the 2000 National Household Survey on Drug Abuse (NHSDA Series: H-13, DHHS Publication No. SMA 01-3549)." 2001. U.S. Department of Health and Human Services. http://www.samhsa.gov/oas/2k2/suicide/suicide.pdf.

Taylor, Elizabeth J., ed. *Dorland's Illustrated Medical Dictionary*. 27th ed. Philadelphia, PA: W. B. Saunders, 1988.

U.S. Department of Transportation, National Highway Traffic Safety Administration. "Traffic Safety Facts 2001: A Compilation of Motor Vehicle Crash Data from the Fatality Analysis Reporting System and the General Estimates System." 2001. http://www-nrd.nhtsa.dot.gov/pdf/nrd-30/NCSA/TSFAnn/TSF2001.pdf.

U.S. Drug Enforcement Administration, "Drug Information" (Washington, D.C.: DEA, n.d.), http://www.justice.gov/dea/concern/concern.html.

Van Cleave, Stephen, Walter Byrd, and Kathy Revell. *Counseling for Substance Abuse and Addiction*. Edited by Gary R. Collins. Resources for Christian Counseling, vol. 12. Dallas: Word, 1987.

VanVonderen, Jeff. *Good News for the Chemically Dependent and Those Who Love Them*. Rev. and updated ed. Nashville: Thomas Nelson, 1991.

The World's Best Anatomical Charts: Diseases and Disorders. Skokie, IL: Anatomical Chart Company, 2000.

June Hunt's HOPE FOR THE HEART minibooks are biblically-based, and full of practical advice that is relevant, spiritually-fulfilling and wholesome.

HOPE FOR THE HEART TITLES

Adultery	ISBN 9781596366848
Alcohol & Drug Abuse	ISBN 9781596366596
Anger	ISBN 9781596366411
Anorexia & Bulimia	ISBN 9781596369313
Bullying	ISBN 9781596369269
Codependency	ISBN 9781596366510
Conflict Resolution	ISBN 9781596366473
Confrontation	ISBN 9781596366886
Considering Marriage	ISBN 9781596366763
Decision Making	ISBN 9781596366534
Depression	ISBN 9781596366497
Domestic Violence	ISBN 9781596366824
Dysfunctional Family	ISBN 9781596369368
Fear	ISBN 9781596366701
Financial Freedom	ISBN 9781596369412
Forgiveness	ISBN 9781596366435
Friendship	ISBN 9781596368828
Gambling	ISBN 9781596366862
Grief	ISBN 9781596366572
Guilt	ISBN 9781596366961
Hope	ISBN 9781596366558
Loneliness	ISBN 9781596366909
Manipulation	ISBN 9781596366749
Marriage	ISBN 9781596368941
Overeating	ISBN 9781596369467
Parenting	ISBN 9781596366725
Perfectionism	ISBN 9781596369214
Reconciliation	ISBN 9781596368897
Rejection	ISBN 9781596366787
Self-Worth	ISBN 9781596366688
Sexual Integrity	ISBN 9781596366947
Singleness	ISBN 9781596368774
Stress	ISBN 9781596368996
Success Through Failure	ISBN 9781596366923
Suicide Prevention	ISBN 9781596366800
Verbal & Emotional Abuse	ISBN 9781596366459

www.aspirepress.com